Global Cities
LOS ANGELES

Nicola Barber
photographs by Adrian Cooper

Evans

Published by
Evans Brothers Limited,
Part of the Evans Publishing Group,
2A Portman Mansions
Chiltern Street
London W1U 6NR

First published 2007
© copyright Evans Brothers Limited

British Library Cataloguing in Publication Data

Barber, Nicola
Los Angeles. - (Global cities)
1. Los Angeles (Calif.) - Juvenile literature
I. Title
979.4'94054

ISBN-10: 0237531232
13-digit ISBN 9780237531232

Designer: Robert Walster, Big Blu Design
Maps and graphics by Martin Darlinson
All photographs are by Adrian Cooper (EASI-Images), except
p.14 © Corbis, p.15 © Peter Turnley/Corbis, p.17 © Lucas
Jackson/Reuters/Corbis and p.53 © Joseph Sohn; ChromoSohn
Inc./Corbis

Series concept and project management EASI –
Educational Resourcing
(info@easi-er.co.uk)

Contents

Living in an urban world

Some time in 2007 the world's population became, for the first time in history, more urban than rural. An estimated 3.3 billion people found themselves living in towns and cities like Los Angeles, and for many the experience of urban living was relatively new. For example, in China, the world's most populous country, the number of people living in urban areas increased from 196 million in 1980 to over 536 million by 2005.

The urban challenge...

This staggering rate of urbanisation (the process by which a country's population becomes concentrated into towns and cities) is being repeated across much of the world and presents us with a complex set of challenges for the twenty-first century. Many of these challenges are local, such as the provision of clean water for expanding urban populations, but others are global in scale. In 2003 an outbreak of the highly contagious respiratory disease SARS demonstrated this as it spread rapidly amongst the populations of well-connected cities across the globe. The amount of pollution generated by urban areas is also a global concern, particularly as urban residents tend to generate more than their rural counterparts.

▲ The City of Los Angeles in relation to California and (inset) its position in the USA.

... and opportunity!

Urban centres, and particularly major cities like Los Angeles, also provide opportunities for improving life at both a local and global scale. Cities concentrate people and allow for efficient forms of mass transport such as subway or light rail networks. Services such as waste collection, recycling, education and health care can all function more efficiently in a city.

Cities are also centres of learning and often the birthplace of new ideas, from innovations in science and technology to new ways of day-to-day living. Cities provide a platform for the celebration of arts and culture and, as their populations become more multicultural, such celebrations are increasingly global in their reach.

▼ The skyscrapers of central (Downtown) Los Angeles.

A global city

Although all urban centres share certain features in common, there are a number of cities in which the challenges and opportunities facing an urban world are particularly condensed. These can be thought of as global cities, cities that in themselves provide a window on the wider world and reflect the challenges of urbanisation, of globalisation, of citizenship and of sustainable development, that face us all. Los Angeles is one such city.

In just over 200 years, the city has grown from a small community of a few hundred people to a vast, sprawling metropolis that is home to one of the most multicultural populations in the world. Immigrants, attracted at first by Los Angeles's location and sunny climate, and later by the discovery of oil and the development of agriculture and industry, have always flocked to the city. Today it is a major hub for shipping, finance, industry and manufacturing. It is also a hugely influential cultural centre, birthplace of the Hollywood movie industry, and home to many outstanding collections of art.

▲ Around half of the area of the City of Los Angeles is hilly or mountainous, restricting space in the city centre.

Defining the city

This book is largely concerned with the City of Los Angeles, often known simply as LA. The city has a population of 3.9 million, and covers a huge area of over 1,200 square kilometres. Over time, as it expanded, the city annexed local farming settlements, for example many of the towns and cities in the San Fernando Valley in the north of the city. Today the city sprawls northwards as far as Sylmar and Granada Hills, and extends southwards to San Pedro and Terminal Island.

Its boundaries are very complicated, as there are areas such as Beverly Hills and West Hollywood, Santa Monica and San Fernando which, although they are surrounded geographically by it, are not part of the City of Los Angeles. The whole area is, however, part of Los Angeles County which covers 10,500 sq km and has a population of over ten million people. The City of Los Angeles is the county seat of government.

Los Angeles also forms part of a vast urban area that is often known as the Greater Los Angeles area (see map on page 8). This area extends over five counties – Los Angeles, Orange, San Bernardino, Riverside and Ventura – and it includes many cities and towns such as Santa Ana, Anaheim, San Bernadino, Long Beach and Palmdale. It has an estimated population of over 18 million people, and a total area of nearly 88,000 sq km.

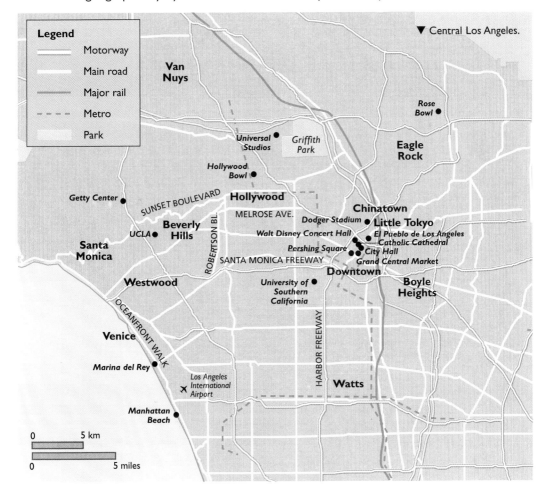

▼ Central Los Angeles.

Legend
- Motorway
- Main road
- Major rail
- Metro
- Park

Van Nuys

Rose Bowl ●

Universal Studios ● Griffith Park

Eagle Rock

Hollywood Bowl ●

Getty Center ●

SUNSET BOULEVARD Hollywood

Chinatown

MELROSE AVE. Dodger Stadium ● Little Tokyo

Beverly Hills

ROBERTSON BL.

Walt Disney Concert Hall El Pueblo de Los Angeles ● Catholic Cathedral

UCLA ●

Santa Monica

Pershing Square ●● City Hall

SANTA MONICA FREEWAY Grand Central Market

Downtown

Westwood

University of Southern California

Boyle Heights

OCEANFRONT WALK

Venice

HARBOR FREEWAY

Marina del Rey ●

Los Angeles International Airport ✕

Watts

Manhattan Beach ●

0   5 km

0   5 miles

The history of Los Angeles

The history of Los Angeles started officially in 1769, when a group of Spanish missionaries and soldiers led by Father Junípero Serra and Gaspar de Portola undertook an exploratory journey through California. One night, they camped in a 'delightful place' by a river. Portola named the river 'El Rio de Nuestra Señora la Reina de los Angeles del Río de Porciúncula' – 'The River of Our Lady the Queen of the Angels of Porciuncula'. In 1771, Serra founded the San Gabriel Mission to form the centre of a new 'community' in the region.

▲The remains of the Mission at San Juan Capistrano, founded by Father Junípero Serra in 1776 and believed to be the oldest building in California.

First peoples

However, these Spanish settlers were not the first inhabitants of the area. Like the rest of the Americas, California had been settled many thousands of years before by ancestors of the Native Americans, and when the Spanish arrived there were already many Native American tribes in the region.

Nevertheless, the Spanish were keen to establish their claim to California, and on 4 September 1781 (the city's official birthdate) a group of settlers from Mexico, which was then under Spanish control, established the first pueblo (settlement) in the 'delightful place' on the river. The pueblo was named after the river, and its name was eventually shortened to Los Angeles.

▲ The City Seal of Los Angeles. The olives, grapes and oranges are a reminder of the city's agricultural heritage.

The early years

By 1790, the settlement had a population of 139, and by 1800 the population had more than doubled to 315. In 1821, Mexico became independent from Spain and took over control of California. But this was the era of expansion for the United States, when the US government adopted a policy known as 'Manifest Destiny'. This was based on the belief that the United States had a duty to extend its borders from the east to the west coast of the continent in order to spread democracy and freedom. In 1846, this expansionist policy led to war between Mexico and the United States, and two years later in the Treaty of Guadalupe Hidalgo, Mexico was forced to hand over California, Arizona and New Mexico to the United States government.

The discovery of gold in 1848 brought hundreds of thousands of people from all over the world to California. A railway linking San Francisco to New York on the east coast was completed in 1869, and in 1876 the railway link was extended to Los Angeles. The trains brought thousands of migrants west to settle in Los Angeles. At the same time, an orange-growing industry was established and in 1892, oil was discovered in the Los Angeles area. The population of Los Angeles expanded rapidly throughout this period, soaring from 1,600 in 1850 to 100,000 in 1900.

▲ Visitors to the Orange Empire Railway Museum in Orange County find out about the history of the Californian railways.

▶ Spanish missionaries were the first to cultivate oranges in Los Angeles.

Water supply

As Los Angeles' population increased, its water supply became a major issue. The city relied on water taken from the river and occasional rainfall, but this was not enough to sustain further expansion. In 1913, an aqueduct was completed to carry water from the Owens River Valley over 320 kilometres to the north of the city. The aqueduct was extended even further north to tap into Mono Lake, high in the Sierra Nevada mountain range, in the 1940s.

Expansion and immigration

With its water supply guaranteed, and its sunny Californian climate, Los Angeles attracted many new businesses, including the movie and aircraft industries in the early twentieth century. Immigration into the city continued, with people coming from all over the world. In the 1860s, many of the labourers from China who had come to work on the railways (see page 13) settled in Los Angeles. By 1900, the city's Chinatown had a population of about 3,000. During the years of the revolutionary wars in Mexico (1910-21) thousands of refugees arrived from Mexico to make new lives in Los Angeles.

During the Great Depression of the 1930s, the catastrophic conditions in the prairie states of the central US sent a wave of desperate and poverty-stricken migrants westwards to look for work in Los Angeles and other west-coast cities. A sizable Japanese population (about 35,000 in the 1930s) was based in the Little Tokyo area of the city. However, during World War II all Japanese Americans who lived in the west-coast states of the United States were interned in so-called 'relocation camps'. In reality, these camps were overcrowded, hastily-built detention centres where medical care was poor. Many Japanese Americans chose not to return to their previous homes after their experiences.

▼ Mexican refugees at a refugee camp in the USA.

▲ An old movie theatre on Broadway, the historic theatre district in Downtown Los Angeles.

Fire and earthquake

Los Angeles is built in a region with little rainfall and subject to tectonic activity. Both wildfires and earthquakes have had a big impact on the city and its inhabitants. In 1993, firestorms swept across southern California, killing four people, destroying properties and making thousands of people homeless. Just a year later, a massive earthquake, measuring 6.7 on the Richter scale, hit the city, killing 57 people and causing more than US$44 billion worth of damage.

Ethnic tensions

Tensions between the many different communities in Los Angeles have periodically risen to the surface during the city's history. As early as 1871, racial violence erupted when 19 Chinese people were murdered by a mob in an incident which became known as the Chinese Massacre. In 1965, the Watts riots erupted in a mostly African-American neighbourhood of the city, and trouble flared again in 1992 as a result of tensions between Hispanic, Korean and African-American communities (see page 20).

▲ Fires burn in South Central Los Angeles in April 1992, lit during the so-called Rodney King Riots (see page 20).

The people of Los Angeles

In 2004, the population of the City of Los Angeles was estimated at 3,845,541, making it the second biggest city in the United States after New York. Its population grew continuously throughout the 20th century, largely due to immigration into the city. Today, Los Angeles has one of the most ethnically diverse populations of anywhere in the world, with people from over 140 different countries resident in the city.

A diverse population

In the 2000 census, the US Census Bureau collected data about the various races that make up the population of Los Angeles. (It did not include Hispanics – see page 17 – as they can be of various races.) The census showed that 46.9 per cent of the population of the city was white, while the African-American population made up 11.2 per cent. The Asian-American population was the next biggest, while Native Americans made up 0.8 per cent and Hawaiian and other Pacific islanders made up 0.2 per cent.

The Asian-American and Hispanic sections of the population are growing particularly rapidly in Los Angeles. From the 1970s onwards, large numbers of people from China, the Philippines, Korea, Vietnam and India have made the city their home.

▲ Mexican musicians perform on Olvera Street, in the historic area of El Pueblo de Los Angeles.

Many were well-educated and have set up successful businesses in the city. The Asian-American population now makes up ten per cent of Los Angeles' population.

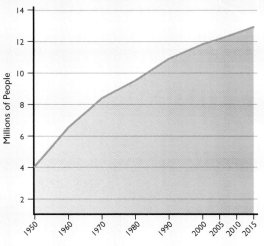

▲ Greater Los Angeles' population growth 1950-2015.

16

Immigration reform

Hispanic is a term used to describe a person of any race who has their origins in the Spanish-speaking countries of Mexico, Central and South America. Today 46.5 per cent of the Los Angeles population is described as Hispanic. Huge numbers of Hispanics have moved to Los Angeles in search of higher-paying jobs and a better quality of life. Historically, much of this migration has taken place illegally across the Mexico-US border and it is estimated that there are up to 12 million illegal immigrants currently residing in the US, mainly concentrated in the southern states of California, Texas and Florida. Most find relatively low-paid employment in agriculture, transport and construction.

In March 2006 there were huge demonstrations in Los Angeles, as over half a million people protested about proposed federal government plans to crack down on illegal immigrants as well as those who employ them, and to build more security walls to prevent people crossing the border between the US and Mexico illegally. Protestors called the proposals 'inhumane', arguing that they target the poorest in society who provide an important source of labour for the US economy. The demonstration was said to be the largest in recent US history.

▼ Protestors gather in their thousands in Downtown LA on 25 March 2006 to protest against proposed crackdowns on illegal immigrants.

Languages

While English is the main language of Los Angeles, the city's large Hispanic population means that Spanish is also very widely spoken across the city. According to the US Census of 2004, of the 61.4 per cent of inhabitants of Los Angeles who speak a language other than English, roughly three quarters speak Spanish. The range of other languages spoken in the city indicates the variety of communities within it – they include Mandarin Chinese and Cantonese, Japanese, Farsi (Persian, as spoken by the Iranian population), Arabic, Armenian, Korean, Vietnamese and Russian. Many people speak more than one language, and in many cases languages are becoming mixed to create 'pidgin' languages unique to certain parts of the city, for example English-Korean or English-Japanese.

Ethnic communities

In many cases, communities from different ethnic backgrounds have settled in particular areas of the city. Chinese immigrants established Chinatown in Downtown (central) Los Angeles in the nineteenth century, and this area of the city remains the heart of the Chinese-American community, although other neighbourhoods such as Monterey Park and San Gabriel also have high percentages of Chinese-American residents. South of Chinatown is Little Tokyo, centre of the Japanese community and home of the Japanese American National Museum. West of Little Tokyo is Koreatown, home to the largest Korean population in the United States. Other areas of the city known for their ethnic communities include Little Armenia, Thai Town and Little Ethiopia.

▼ People enjoy a Japanese meal in Little Tokyo.

A city of extremes

Like most cities, Los Angeles has extremes of wealth and poverty. Some of the richest and most famous people in the world live in the mansions of West Hollywood, Beverly Hills and Bel Air. But in many neighbourhoods of the city people live in overcrowded and dilapidated tenement buildings, which have been divided up to provide low-cost apartments. Some of the poorest people in the city are found on Skid Row, an area in Downtown Los Angeles. The inhabitants of Skid Row live on the streets in tents and cardboard boxes. It is estimated that around 8,000 people live in these conditions.

▲ One of the many exclusive homes that line the roads of Beverly Hills.

▲ Typical low-quality housing in southeast Los Angeles.

CASE STUDY

Joyce Perkins, Executive Director, (LANI)

The Los Angeles Neighbourhood Initiative (LANI) was founded in 1994 to help communities improve their neighbourhoods. It has many projects throughout the city, including in Koreatown and Little Ethiopia.

Joyce explains: "It all began because there was a traffic issue in my neighbourhood. I started a petition and managed to get the problems solved. In 1993 I was invited to write a proposal for a bus-stop program with a fund of US$2.5million to improve bus facilities in the city. To administer this research project I set up a non-profit organisation. And now, here we are with LANI. It is my passion: making sure communities have a say in the development of transport, schools, and so on. After that first project we were given the nod from City Hall to create a model for hands-on development. We would handle the design, the budget, the construction and the reports for projects.

One of the big issues for neighbour-hoods is the lack of green spaces. There is a shortage in LA. We have done a number of projects we call 'pocket parks' which restore redundant spaces. These spaces are often on busy transit routes in the city. By planting trees, creating small gardens, we attract small businesses like restaurants and coffee shops. This attracts people and improves the overall atmosphere of a place, making areas safer to be in, more friendly. We help to improve pavements, bus stops, green spaces – then local business and residents do the rest.

The simple fact is City Hall can't afford to do everything, so non-profit groups like us and people in communities who volunteer their time are critical in the future development of the city."

The Rodney King riots

Los Angeles' multiethnic population gives the city a vibrant and cosmopolitan atmosphere, and its mixture of cultures is one of the city's greatest strengths. However, race-related incidents inevitably occur, and occasionally such incidents have sparked off violence. The trigger for the riots of 1992 (see page 15) was the not-guilty verdict in the trial of four police officers accused of beating an African-American motorist called Rodney King the previous year. However, the violence was also the result of long-standing tensions between local communities. The riots lasted for several days and between 50 and 60 people died during the violence.

Crime and the police

The Los Angeles Police Department (LAPD) is famous worldwide from its

▲ A recruitment drive for the LAPD.

▼ A policeman in Downtown Los Angeles. The LAPD was established in 1869.

depictions in many television shows and films. Some of its officers have been accused of racial discrimination against ethnic minorities in the city. In the 1990s, the LAPD became caught up in controversy as a result of the Rodney King riots, and in 1999 the so-called Rampart scandal broke, when police officers were accused of making up evidence and dealing drugs. Due to decades of underfunding, the LAPD has one of the lowest ratios of police officers to population of any of the major cities of the United States – for example, half the number of police per capita compared to New York. It also has to deal with Los Angeles' large population of criminal, often warring, gangs. It is estimated that there are over 400 gangs in Los Angeles, predominantly made up of African-Americans or Hispanics, although there is also a growing Asian-American gang population in the city. More than half the homicides committed each year in the city are gang-related.

Religion in Los Angeles

A wide array of religions are practised by the people of Los Angeles. The city has a large Roman Catholic population, and a new Catholic cathedral was completed in 2002 in the city to replace an earlier building that had been damaged in the earthquake of 1994. There are many Protestant Christian denominations within the city, including Baptists and other evangelical movements. Also part of the wider Christian Church is the Church of Jesus Christ of Latter-day Saints, also known as the Mormon Church.

Los Angeles is home to the second-largest Jewish community in the United States (after New York). It also has significant Muslim, Buddhist and Hindu populations, and there are many mosques and temples in the city. The Buddhist Hsi Lai temple is the biggest in the United States. The religion of Scientology, founded in the 1950s by the author L. Ron Hubbard, had its first church in Los Angeles. Today there is a large Scientology centre in the city, with high-profile followers including actors Tom Cruise and John Travolta.

▶ Residents in Santa Monica celebrate the Jewish festival of Chanukah.

▼ Arriving for prayers in one of Los Angeles' many mosques, Masjid Ibadullah on W. Jefferson Boulevard.

Living in Los Angeles

The actor and director Woody Allen once said of Los Angeles that it is 'a suburb in search of a city'. The city is already vast, sprawling across a total of around 1,200 sq km and over the years its residents have been forced further out from the city centre, resulting in heavy traffic and ever longer commutes. The rapid growth in the population of the city through the twentieth century resulted in residential development spreading out from the central districts to cover areas such as the San Fernando Valley to the north. As it grew, Los Angeles also annexed nearby towns and cities such as Hollywood. Nevertheless, the city has a high average population density at 3,260 people per sq km.

▲ Typical housing in the vast suburbs of Los Angeles.

Local geography

The geography of the City of Los Angeles has shaped its growth over the years. About 45 per cent of the city's land area is hilly or mountainous. The San Gabriel Mountains lie to the east of the city, while the Santa Monica Mountains divide the Los Angeles basin from the San Fernando Valley to the north. Onshore breezes from the Pacific Ocean blow the city's smog and pollution inland, where it becomes trapped by the surrounding mountains. This has led to the western, relatively pollution-free districts of the city being favoured by Los Angeles' more affluent residents, while the east and south are home to poorer neighbourhoods.

Housing crisis

Housing for the city's expanding population is a major issue in Los Angeles. A very large proportion of people in Los Angeles rent rather than own their homes. Studies have shown that people who rent tend to come from low-income groups, pay a higher proportion of their incomes towards their housing and are more likely to live in substandard conditions. However, in recent years the cost of renting, and of buying a home in Los Angeles has rocketed, while wages in the city have not followed suit.

▶ These buildings are part of a low-cost housing project in Downtown Los Angeles.

Task force

In 1999, the Los Angeles City Council became so concerned about the levels of housing prices in the city, and the resulting effect upon the economy, that it commissioned a Housing Crisis Task Force made up of council members, business and community

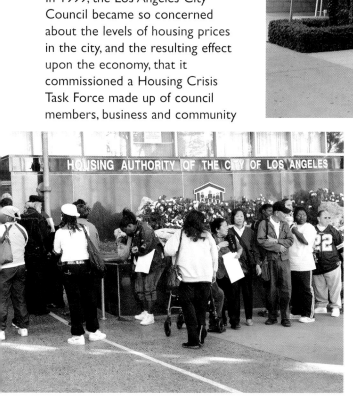

leaders. Federal guidelines state that for housing to be 'affordable' it should use up no more than 30 per cent of income in rent or other payments. However, the Task Force found that in order to afford an average two-bedroom apartment, a worker on the Californian minimum wage of US$5.75 an hour would have to work more than 100 hours a week, just to pay the rent.

◀ A queue forms at the Los Angeles Housing Authority, which offers support to those on a low income.

Affordable housing

Lack of affordable housing in Los Angeles means that many poor people live in overcrowded and substandard accommodation, or in places that were not intended for human habitation such as converted garages. The census of 2000 found that 26 per cent of all households in Los Angeles were overcrowded. Some people lose their homes because they cannot afford to pay their rent, and in 2005, it was estimated that up to 47,000

▲ Homeless people queue for a meal at a volunteer-run service in Santa Monica.

people were homeless on any night in Los Angeles. People on middle incomes who want to buy a home are forced to move to distant suburbs in Los Angeles County.

The city council, together with many local organisations and businesses, is working to try to improve the situation by increasing the availability of high-quality affordable housing in many areas of the city. There are, however, major problems to be overcome. The gap is wide between market rents and the amount people can actually afford to pay. Plans for new, affordable housing schemes are often treated with suspicion by existing residents of a neighbourhood. New development schemes also require services such as sewerage, shopping and transport facilities and schools. Nevertheless innovatory projects are underway, for example developing industrial and commercial premises into residential developments, renovating old and abandoned buildings, and encouraging mixed-use zones – where developers build a mix of commercial and residential units.

◀ Old office blocks and warehouses in Downtown Los Angeles have recently become fashionable – and expensive – places to live.

Sam Mistrano, Deputy Director of SCANPH

The Southern California Association of Non-Profit Housing (SCANPH) is a non-profit housing association dedicated to developing affordable housing for low-income families.

Sam: "SCANPH changes policy to help southern Californian property developers build low-cost housing. I've been working at SCANPH for four years now.

There is a myth that says if you work your life will be secure and successful. This myth demonises the poor and those on low income. It says to them: you're poor because you don't work hard enough. This is wrong. Los Angeles has a fluid population and there is less structure for people to be grounded. And you won't really see the poverty here – it's hidden. The overcrowding is all around us though – Downtown high rises, places with four families living in one home. What has happened is that house prices have gone through the roof in the last four years. An average home has gone from US$225,000 to US$475,000. Rents, too, have gone by up to 30 per cent a year. This affects everyone: rich kids stay at home longer, unable to afford a first home. Working-class people and immigrants live in overcrowded buildings."

This graph shows the correlation between areas of employment and average annual salary and rate of home ownership among residents of Los Angeles. It is becoming increasingly difficult for low-earning workers to afford their own homes. Campaigns by organisations like SCANPH (see case study) aim to help create more low-cost housing for these workers.

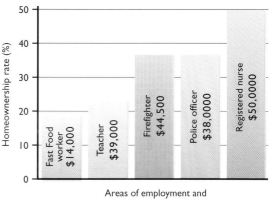

Areas of employment and average income

Schools

Most schools in Los Angeles are run by the Los Angeles Unified School District (LAUSD). Since the late 1970s, lack of funding for many city schools has been a problem, and the LAUSD has acquired a reputation for overcrowded and rundown schools, where violence and petty crime have become increasingly common.

Wealthy parents have traditionally avoided LAUSD schools by paying for private education for their children. However, new initiatives to improve school premises and relieve overcrowding have helped many schools, and the LAUSD is targeting areas such as literacy and mathematics to try to raise standards for all. The LAUSD also has its

▲ A Los Angeles school bus.

own police force, dedicated entirely to creating a safe and tranquil environment for students, teachers and staff. The police force deals with violence in schools, as well as drug- and alcohol-related offences.

▼ High school students at an LAUSD school.

Kelly Hancock and Maura Claire Draheim, teachers

Kelly Hancock teaches English, and Maura Claire Draheim teaches Social Studies, at James Monroe High School, an LAUSD school in the North Hills district of Los Angeles. Ninety per cent of the students at the school are Hispanic.

Kelly explains "The biggest problem with schools in LA is overcrowding, especially in urban schools. There are also levels of violence and lack of family support for students. There is a large immigrant population here in LA, which means that close to 50 per cent of people in schools are at a 'learner' English level, English isn't their first language. At our school there are 5,000 students. It's so big that we are broken into smaller 'communities'.

We have been working on something called a 'core class'. It is a model between Maura and myself, which means we share

▲ Maura Claire Draheim (left) and Kelly Hancock.

some core students and overlap our lessons. For example, if Maura is teaching the First World War, I'll teach the poets of the First World War.

It also goes outside the classroom. We asked our students what the problems were in their own communities. They said gangs and trash. We developed the idea of clear-up programmes, inviting different speakers into the school to talk about what sort of techniques we could use to create our own projects. We also made a documentary film about a street clear-up."

Higher education

Los Angeles is home to both publicly and privately funded higher education institutions. The largest of the universities in terms of number of students is the University of California, Los Angeles (UCLA). UCLA is publicly funded. Also found in the city is the University of Southern California (USC), a privately funded university renowned worldwide for its research programs. There are many other universities and colleges in the city, such as Pepperdine University and the Los Angeles Trade Technical College.

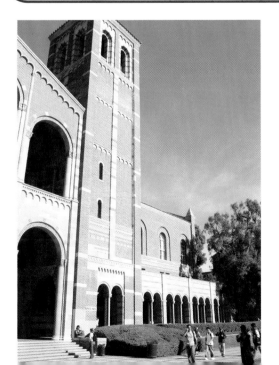

◄ The UCLA campus in western Los Angeles.

27

Health

Healthcare in the United States is paid for through private insurance, often through an employer's health insurance scheme. For those who cannot afford health insurance, or who do not receive insurance as part of their employment package, the government-funded Medicaid may cover some health care costs. However, many people neither have insurance nor qualify for Medicaid. According to figures published by the Department of Health Services, 13.5 per cent of adults in Los Angeles County could not afford to see a doctor when they needed to in 2002-3.

A major health issue is obesity; a recent report (2003) indicated that over half of all adults, and up to a quarter of all children in Los Angeles County are either obese or overweight. Obesity increases the risk of developing many serious illnesses including

heart disease. Coronary heart disease is currently one of the leading causes of death in Los Angeles County, accounting for a total of one in four deaths. Obesity is also implicated in diabetes and many types of cancer. Poor diet and lack of activity are the main causes of obesity, and the problem is starting to be tackled in the county's schools by measures such as the removal of machines selling sweet, fizzy drinks.

Los Angeles weather

The climate of Los Angeles has always been one of the great attractions of the city. The winter months (December to March) are rainy, although the rain is often followed by days of blue skies. Temperatures can dip down to 9°C. The springtime is warmer with less rain, and the summer months (June to August) are pleasantly hot, with temperatures up to 29°C. However, cold fog often rolls over the city in the evenings, and smog is often at its worst in these months. The autumn months are very pleasant, with clear skies and little fog.

▲ Fast food is a major factor in high levels of obesity.

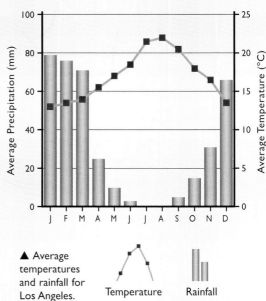

▲ Average temperatures and rainfall for Los Angeles.

Temperature   Rainfall

Out and about in Los Angeles

Los Angeles is so huge, and made up of so many different neighbourhoods, each with its own character, that it is not surprising that its residents have a vast choice of places to go for shopping, eating and drinking. The city's cosmopolitan mix of cultures is reflected in the wide variety of shops across the city – from the ultra-chic and expensive boutiques on Robertson Boulevard to the stalls selling cheap knick-knacks along Ocean Front Walk. Areas such as Chinatown and Little Tokyo cater for the local Chinese and Japanese populations with specialist supermarkets and grocery stores.

Farmers' markets

Los Angeles is famous for its farmers' markets which sell fresh and seasonal produce direct from the grower. The first farmers' market was set up in 1934 on some empty land known as Gilmore Island in West Hollywood. This original market is still going, and is famous worldwide, but there are many others scattered across the city. Most are weekly markets and people flock to them to buy fresh fruit and vegetables, cheeses, baked goods, herbs, meats and seafood.

▲ A farmers' market in Santa Monica, where people can buy fresh, local and organic produce.

The beach

Los Angeles' sunny weather, and its location ensure that beach life is a vital part of the lifestyle of many of its residents. Families, swimmers, board surfers and windsurfers alike head down to Santa Monica, Zuma and Manhattan beaches. The Ocean Front Walk in Venice is the place where street performers enthrall the crowds, and muscle men work out at the open-air gym.

▲ The white sands of Venice Beach.

The Los Angeles economy

The wealth of Los Angeles was originally built on agriculture and oil production. The opening of the Owens Valley Aqueduct in 1913 (see page 14) was a key moment in the city's history, as it provided the water supplies to support the ever-growing population necessary for the city's economic expansion. Early in the twentieth century the movie industry became established in the city, attracted largely by the sunny climate of California which made filming outdoors possible for much of the year. The aerospace and defence industries also developed during the twentieth century and became a vital part of the city's economy.

▶ A 'nodding donkey' pumps oil to the surface near El Porto.

Manufacturing

Today, Los Angeles is the largest manufacturing centre in the United States, employing approximately 470,400 people (the next biggest employer is Chicago with 396,000), and producing a variety of goods such as clothing and textiles, toys, computers and software, electrical and pharmaceutical products.

Many Los Angeles-based companies now rely on labour from immigrant communities, particularly migrants from Mexico and other Central American countries. However, in recent years some companies have moved their manufacturing centres across the border to Mexico, or abroad to Asian countries such as China, to take advantage of cheaper labour and production costs.

▶ A worker in a Los Angeles textile factory making baseball kits (see case study, page 31).

Steve Due, Production and Manufacturing Coordinator for Custom Athletic Uniforms

"This company is a niche company, and that's why we've survived, still manufacturing while a lot of the industry has left for Asia and China. It's an ongoing process. During the Industrial Revolution lots of jobs around the world were lost to this country. America has done well for many, many years: now it's somebody else's turn for a while. But when it gets too expensive in China, production will move to Bangladesh – manufacturing will make its trip around the world. Nobody in the US gets a job for life anymore. With our custom-made stuff, we're fine. Our quality has to be better – if not we'd be out of business. I enjoy doing this. A lot of people don't get the chance to stay in one area of work for many years: I'm lucky."

◀ Custom Athletic Uniforms is a niche company that makes kits for baseball players.

Gateway to the world

The port of Los Angeles is the busiest in the United States, handling around US$148.5 billion of cargo in 2004, and one of the most important in the world. Although the port was officially opened in 1907, its importance increased rapidly after the opening of the Panama Canal in 1914, as it was the closest large US port to the canal. Today it plays a vital role in Pacific-Rim trade, its top five trading partners being China, Japan, Taiwan, Thailand and South Korea. It is a vital component in the economy of Los Angeles, employing nearly 17,000 people, and providing a gateway for both exporting and importing goods. Main imports include furniture, clothing and vehicles, while exports include paper, fabrics and fruit and vegetables.

▼ Freight is loaded on to a ship at Los Angeles port.

The service sector

In recent years the service sector has become increasingly important in the economy of Los Angeles, including areas such as financial services, health care, construction, education and transportation. Tourism is also an important aspect of the service industry in the city, supporting businesses such as hotels and restaurants.

Other 33%

Services 33%

Manufacturing 12%

Wholesale & Retail 22%

◄ A pie chart showing employment by sector in Los Angeles.

▲ Taxis wait for custom in the financial district of Downtown Los Angeles.

Entertainment industry

The entertainment industry, covering movie, television and recording companies, remains a huge and very important employer in Los Angeles, providing jobs for around 160,000 people. The city is home to many world-famous names including Twentieth-Century Fox and Paramount Pictures. It is also the headquarters of Univision, the largest Spanish-language television network in the United States. The city is such a popular location for making movies and television programmes that, in 1995, the City and County of Los Angeles agreed jointly to set up an independent organisation to deal with companies who wanted to film on location in the County. FilmL.A. Inc issues film permits and liaises between film companies and communities whose neighbourhoods may be disrupted by filming activities.

▼ A film crew at work in Downtown Los Angeles.

▲ The entrance to the Paramount Pictures film studio in Hollywood.

CASE STUDY

John Romano, screenwriter and executive producer

"I'm from New Jersey originally. I had some friends in theatre in New York who eventually went into television and asked me to write some shows called Hill Street Blues. I did that and soon realised I had to be in LA if I wanted to make a living as a writer. You just have to move to LA. Even if you're a waiter here you've more chance of working in television or the movies than if you go to film school somwhere else. In other places people dream of making movies, in LA it is real and daily. So I moved here with my family.

I started in television, which is much more a writer's medium than film. Writing for TV is a regular job. Every morning I would commute to a little studio lot. First thing we used to do – there were five or six writers in a team – was sit and cook up stories in the writer's room. At the beginning of a season, in June or July, we would plot out the entire year, using cards and boards to map out what would happen to all the characters. By the end of August we would be shooting one episode, writing the next and editing another all at the same time. It was very intense.

In the movies things are different. They don't really have a schedule. I wrote one film that took nine years to make it to the screen. Now I don't write for television I have a lot more time to develop ideas and stories."

Wealth and poverty in Los Angeles

The City of Los Angeles went through a period of recession in the early 1990s, as thousands of jobs were lost in manufacturing and unemployment rates climbed as high as ten per cent. Although the unemployment figure has now roughly halved, economic growth has not been evenly spread across the city, and the gap between the rich and the poor has been steadily growing. From 1990 to 2000, the average household income in Los Angeles decreased, compared to an average increase in California and across the United States generally. According to the US Census of 2000, the percentage of families living below poverty level in Los Angeles was 15.8 per cent in 1999, compared to a US average of 10.1 per cent.

The income gap

The widening of the income gap between rich and poor is largely the result of the decrease in manufacturing jobs in Los Angeles, and California as a whole, in the 1990s. These occupations traditionally provided decent wages for middle- and low-income families. They have been replaced with an increase in jobs at both the top and bottom ends of the city's economy. Along with a growth in high-paying jobs in the entertainment and high-tech industries came a surge in low-skill, low-paying jobs largely in the service and retail sectors. However, while the demand for people to work as salespeople, waiters, cleaners, security guards and cashiers has increased, all of these jobs offer low hourly rates of pay. At the same time the cost of living and of housing in Los Angeles has gone up rapidly (see pages 22-24).

▼ A busy lunchtime at a restaurant in the financial district.

The informal economy

One of the fastest growing areas of the economy in Los Angeles is the 'informal economy'. This phrase is used to describe a wide range of jobs for which workers receive wages in cash. The growth of the informal economy is a huge problem for the city, as large amounts of tax revenue are being lost – taxes are rarely deducted from undocumented cash payments. It is also a social problem, as the majority of people employed in this sector are poor, often illegal, immigrants who are often driven by desperation to take on such work. Work in the informal sector typically includes jobs in construction, private household services, restaurants and other food industries, and cleaning services. It is estimated that around 16 per cent of the city's labour force currently works in the informal sector.

▶ A street vendor hopes to make a few dollars at Venice Beach.

Campaigning for a 'living wage'

One organisation that fights for the rights of low-paid workers in Los Angeles is the Los Angeles Alliance for New Economy (LAANE). Its biggest victory came in 1997, when LAANE led a successful campaign to introduce a 'living wage' law in the city of Los Angeles. This law ensured that employees who worked for companies that benefited from contracts with the city council were paid a decent wage, often including health insurance.

◀ A fair wage demonstration outside the luxurious Beverly Wiltshire Hotel.

Los Angeles County covers 10,577 sq km and has the largest population of any county in the United States, with a population of over ten million in 2005. It makes up nearly 28 per cent of the population of California. The county includes within its boundaries 88 cities, each of which has its own city council, and with 3.8 million inhabitants Los Angeles is by far the biggest of these cities.

The City Council

The city is governed by a mayor and a 15-member Council, elected every four years. The Council members represent the 15 different districts into which the city is divided. Other elected officials are the City Controller (chief accounting officer) and City Attorney (legal advisor). The Council is split into 15 committees to cover specific areas, and each council member is the chairperson of one committee and a member of two others. The committees report back to the Council.

▲ City Hall in Downtown Los Angeles.

▲ Just one area the City Council is responsible for is highway maintenance.

The mayor

The mayor is an important figure in the life of Los Angeles, elected for a term of four years and limited to two terms in office. He or she submits proposals to the Council, and has the power to approve or veto laws passed by it. In May 2005, Antonio Villaraigosa was elected as Los Angeles' mayor, defeating his fellow Democrat James Hahn by a large majority. Villaraigosa is Los Angeles' first Hispanic mayor since 1872, and was born and brought up in the city. He has tackled issues such as traffic congestion by banning all roadworks during rush hour in the city. He has also placed a high priority on improving the city's schools (see page 26), tackling homelessness and resolving the housing crisis (see page 23).

Services

The mayor and council are in charge of running many vital services for the city including the police force (the Los Angeles Police Department – see p.20), firefighting, refuse collection and disposal, wastewater collection and treatment, street maintenance, traffic management, public libraries, parks, housing and planning. The Los Angeles Department of Water and Power provides electricity and water supplies to the city, and is the largest municipal utility in the United States.

Many people in Los Angeles feel that the city is too huge to be run by a central body, and that many services should be controlled at a more local level. At its most extreme, this has led to some parts of the city trying to leave Los Angeles altogether to establish themselves as entirely separate places – a movement known as secession (see page 38).

▲ The Los Angeles Council looks after the city's parks.

▼ A refuse collection truck empties waste bins in Santa Monica.

For secession...

In 2002 the districts of San Fernando Valley and Hollywood both attempted to break away from the control of the City of Los Angeles in order to form city units of their own. Dissatisfaction with schools and other public services have long been issues in the San Fernando Valley, and organised attempts to secede date back to the 1960s. In 1977, the California state legislature gave city governments the power to veto secession, but this veto was repealed in 1997, opening the way for new calls for secession. A Los Angeles County commission found that the San Fernando Valley paid out US$127.7 million more in taxes than it received in city services. In 2002, the secession question was finally put to the test through a city-wide vote.

▼ Hollywood was one of the areas that attempted to break away from the control of Los Angeles City.

▶ The Eagle Rock City Hall. Eagle Rock is one of several districts in Los Angeles that have debated the issue of secession.

...and against

The campaign against secession was led by the then mayor of Los Angeles, James Hahn. He argued that splitting Los Angeles up would result in worse services and higher taxes. The mayor was able to call on powerful support to back his view – of the US$10.6 million spent on the secession campaign, US$7.4 million was donated by those opposed to secession, while the San Fernando Valley and Hollywood campaigns jointly raised less than half that amount. The result was that secession for Hollywood was defeated even in Hollywood itself, with 68.5 per cent of residents voting against it, while in the San Fernando Valley 50.7 per cent of residents voted for secession. However, it was the city-wide vote that decided the issue, and 66.9 per cent of voters rejected secession for the San Fernando Valley, and 71.4 per cent rejected it for Hollywood.

Many people in the San Fernando Valley remain determined to continue the campaign. They say that promises made before the vote by Mayor Hahn to repair streets, put up new street lights, and renovate libraries and parks were soon broken, and that dissatisfaction with the City government remains as high as ever.

Charter reform

In 1999, residents in Los Angeles approved a new city charter (a list of its guiding principles), which was adopted in 2000. The reform of the charter was prompted in part by the growing movement for secession, and by a perceived need to involve local communities more closely in the running of the city. As a result, one of the main reforms to the charter included the setting up of a Department of Neighborhood Empowerment to oversee the creation of Neighborhood Councils (see page 40) across the city. The mission statement of the department is: 'To promote public participation in government and make government more responsive to local needs by creating, nurturing, and supporting a citywide system of grass-roots, independent, and participatory Neighborhood Councils.'

▲ This former hotel, The Ambassador, in Downtown LA is being converted into a school to cope with dissatisfaction with the provision of schooling. This was a major issue in the decision of San Fernando Valley and Hollywood to try for secession in 2002.

Neighborhood councils

Neighborhood Councils are made up of groups of people from a particular neighbourhood who are certified or endorsed by the Board of Neighborhood Commissioners. Once certified, they appoint their own leaders, hold elections and determine their own agendas. The City Council gives Neighborhood Councils notification of any issues or projects that may be of particular interest or concern, so that the councils can respond.

The power of the councils was first demonstrated in 2004, when objections from 30 Neighborhood Councils to a proposed 18 per cent increase in water rates by the Department of Water and Power forced the department to reconsider. Neighborhood Councils are

▲ Filming can be a nuisance to local communities.

also increasingly involved in aspects of city life such as building new schools, issues arising from filming on location (see page 32) and the city budget, which is controlled by the mayor. Neighborhood Councils are also active in organising local events and improving local environments.

▼ A family enjoys the amenities of Macarthur Park.

Ken Draper, Citywatch Media Group and Mid-City West Community Council

Ken explains: "The City of Los Angeles delivered reform in a charter in 1999. There were two key issues in it. First, it gave the mayor of LA more power, and left the city councillors with less. The second thing was creating the Neighborhood Councils, for different neighborhoods to have a voice. Now NCs are a layer of government. There isn't a community or council meeting which doesn't include NCs – they always have some input. The NCs' point of greatest influence was two years ago when the Department of Power and Water decided to raise its rates (see page 40). The NCs forced them to sit round the table to discuss this.

Each NC has a standard set of electoral procedures. An NC can run an election in any way it wants, however many times it wants in a year. Each NC can make up its own rules so long as they fit in with the general NC guidelines. My NC, for example, has an election once a year in June. Those who want to be nominated for the NC board publicise their interest and then have to be verified by stakeholders of any given area. The number of stakeholders varies from area to area. It also varies depending on the issue being discussed. My NC has 65,000 stakeholders.

Today I'm at City Hall to discuss Emergency Preparedness. We want to establish a network between different NCs in LA in event of terror, earthquake or flood. NCs are a logical focal point for any community, and our objective is to connect our NC network with the emergency services."

Transport in Los Angeles

Los Angeles is famous worldwide as the city where the car is king. In fact, Los Angeles once had an efficient public transport system consisting of streetcars and electric trains, but both systems were dismantled in the 1940s and 50s. Today Los Angeles has an extensive freeway system that handles millions of commuters every day. The widespread use of the car has contributed to the urban sprawl that characterises the city, as well as being a major cause of the city's air pollution problems.

▶ An old Los Angeles tram, preserved at the Orange Empire Railway Museum.

Travel by car

After Los Angeles' public transport system was dismantled in the 1940s and 50s, a network of high-speed freeways was developed in its place. In many cases, these roads were constructed through the poorer neighbourhoods of the city, for example Boyle Heights. Today, the average commute in Los Angeles is approximately 15 miles, and the length of time people spend commuting by car has increased 60 per cent within the last 10 years. However, it is almost impossible to add to the city's freeway system because of environmental concerns, and because of the difficulties of planning new routes through an already overcrowded city.

◀ Traffic fills the Pasadena Freeway.

Carpool initiatives

The emphasis for the future, therefore, is to make more efficient use of the existing freeway network. The number of carpool lanes is to be increased across the city – these are lanes for the use of cars carrying two or more people only. Commuters are encouraged to share their cars to and from work or school through a dedicated website that helps people to find other commuters doing similar journeys in their own neighbourhoods. In addition, new technology will help to monitor 'choke points' on the city's freeways – points at which traffic converges and slows or stops. In some places, special 'connector' lanes are to be constructed to allow transit and carpool vehicles to move from freeway to freeway without having to change lane, which will also help to ease congestion on the city's busy roads.

▲ A Metrolink train. Metrolink operates across southern California.

Travel by bus and train

The Los Angeles County Metropolitan Transportation Authority (MTA) is responsible for public transport across the whole of Los Angeles County, including bus, light rail and subway systems. There are four Metro rail lines and over 200 bus lines.

In 1996, MTA was accused in a court case of investing disproportionately in rail lines that favoured white communities in Los Angeles, rather than bus services that tended to serve low-income, minority neighbourhoods. In the settlement that followed, MTA agreed to invest over US$5 billion over the next ten years in the city's bus services. New air-conditioned buses which are 18 metres long and have an 'accordion' middle, allowing them to bend, are now being introduced in the city.

◄ A passenger studies a Metrolink map at a suburban station.

Future plans

The Los Angeles County Metropolitan Transportation Authority plans to continue the expansion of public transport in the county in the future. As well as investing in new bus lines and extending existing rail lines, there will be new emphasis on trying to encourage greater use of public transport. The use of bus lanes to move buses past slow-moving traffic, and high-capacity buses to carry larger numbers of passengers are two important parts of this plan. Ease of use of public transport is another vital element – a universal fare system that will allow passengers to use buses, trains and subways interchangeably is one part of this strategy. Increased use of public transport, as well as being a more sustainable solution to travelling around the city, will also have the added benefit of being good for the environment, as less traffic on the roads will lead to a reduction in air pollution.

▼ One of Los Angeles' new buses. It has a bicycle rack to allow cyclists to use the bus network.

LAX

Los Angeles has five major commercial airports, but Los Angeles International (LAX) is the city's main airport. It is one of the busiest in the world, and is the third busiest in the United States (after Hartsfield Airport in Atlanta and O'Hare Airport in Chicago), handling over 60 million passengers in 2005. The airport is also important for movement of freight, but adds pressure to the road system around Los Angeles as freight is then transported by heavy goods vehicles. Major improvements are planned for the airport in the future, including noise mitigation, traffic management and landscaping, and the airport authorities have been working closely with the local community to agree the best way forward for the LAX Master Plan which lays out the future development of the airport.

▲ Traffic heads towards Los Angeles Airport.

Tressie Kwon, bus operator for the MTA

"I started driving for Metro (see page 43) in 2002. I'm familiar with every route that this particular division covers but I have about three routes that I cover during the week. They always start here, at the depot.

The worse thing about driving is the traffic. It starts at about 6 am and stops at 9 pm. Traffic is always heavy during the day. The congestion is a lot worse than when I started, three years ago. It can be very frustrating because I have a schedule to keep and if you get stuck for four blocks it knocks off the whole schedule. And the passengers get angry because of it, so it does get a little stressful. But I cope. My personal philosophy is: I do the best I can. I try to explain to people what's going on, why I'm late.

I like my job. I love the diversity in the city. It's different every day. You meet some great people – and sometimes you meet some not so great people. I like the variety the job offers. I also love LA. I can be at the beach in 15 minutes. I meet people from all over the world here."

▼ Tressie has seen traffic congestion in Los Angeles worsen in the three years she has worked for the MTA.

Culture, leisure and tourism

Los Angeles is a world centre for culture. Cinemas, concert halls, museums and theatres all offer a wide variety of world-class entertainment for residents and visitors alike. Los Angeles also boasts some stunning architecture, with landmark buildings ranging from the nineteenth-century Bradbury Building in Downtown to masterpieces by architect Frank Lloyd Wright, and from the three-storey pair of binoculars of the Chiat/Day Building to the striking Walt Disney Concert Hall designed by Frank Gehry, which opened in 2003.

The performing arts

Los Angeles has its own world-famous symphony orchestra, the Los Angeles Philharmonic, which performs at the Walt Disney Concert Hall and at an open-air amphitheatre called the Hollywood Bowl. It also hosts a world-class opera company, the Los Angeles Opera, which has as its director the star tenor Plácido Domingo. There is a wide range of theatres, including the Will Geer Theatricum Botanicum, an open-air amphitheatre that lies in the Santa Monica Mountains. Big-name and less famous comedy stars alike perform at clubs such as the Comedy Store. Pop and rock music stars appear at venues such as the Staples Center, a huge sports and entertainment arena in Downtown, the Hollywood Bowl or the Universal Amphitheatre.

▼ The Los Angeles Opera performs here at the Dorothy Chandler Pavilion.

The movies

Not surprisingly, in a city where the movie industry is so important, there is a wide choice of cinemas in Los Angeles. One of the most famous is Grauman's Chinese Theater which has hosted countless movie premiers since it opened in 1927. The Silent Movie Theater is the only cinema in the United States devoted entirely to silent movies. There are also many open-air cinemas in Los Angeles, for example the Santa Monica Drive-In and Cinespia. The movie industry also provides a big draw for tourists, with many studios offering tours. The biggest is the theme park at Universal Studios in Hollywood, which has more than five million visitors every year. Inside the huge park, people can tour a working studio, meet some of the dinosaurs from *Jurassic Park,* and see some spectacular stunts.

▶ The massive Universal Studios theme park attracts millions of visitors a year.

Museums

Los Angeles has huge numbers of museums, most notably the Getty Center in the Santa Monica Mountains and the Museum of Contemporary Art (MOCA). The Getty Center is home to some of the most famous paintings in the world, housed in a beautiful hilltop building designed by Richard Meier. MOCA also has one of the finest art collections in the world, including Japanese and Islamic masterpieces. Other highlights include the Huntington Library with its collection of rare manuscripts, and the historic centre of the city, El Pueblo de Los Angeles, a collection of the oldest surviving buildings in the city.

◀ The Los Angeles County Museum of Art (LACMA).

Tourism

Los Angeles' cultural attractions, its long association with the glamorous movie industry and its sunny climate are all features that help to attract millions of tourists to the city every year. In 2005, 24.9 million visitors came to the city, generating a total of US$12.7 billion for the city's economy. It is the second most popular destination in the United

▲ The view along the front at Venice Beach.

States after New York City for visitors from abroad, and the fourth most popular for domestic tourists after Las Vegas, Orlando and Miami. It is estimated that tourism is the second largest industry in Los Angeles County, providing employment for 260,000 people.

As well as its cultural activities, many visitors come to Los Angeles to visit the beaches, and to shop in the glitzy shops frequented by movie stars in places such as Rodeo Drive. More unusual destinations include the Page Museum at the La Brea Tar Pits in Hollywood, site of more than one million fossilised bones from prehistoric animals. Many visitors to LA have also

◀ Life-size replicas of extinct mammals are among the attractions at the La Brea Tar Pits.

come to visit one of the biggest attractions in the United States for tourists – Disneyland. The world-famous theme park lies south of the Los Angeles County boundary, in Orange County, and attracted a record total of 14.5 million visitors in 2005, when it also celebrated its 50th anniversary.

▶ Tourists and day-trippers gather at the entrance to Disneyland Park.

CASE STUDY

Robin McClain, Media Relations Manager, LA Inc. Convention and Visitors Bureau

"I've lived in LA for six years. When I moved to LA I landed a job in City Hall, working for a councillor as a press deputy. It was a very useful introduction into how the city works, and what it needs to thrive. Not just in politics, but in economic development too. I started working here, at LA Inc, next.

Visitors are seen as very important in LA because of the money they spend. The more time they spend in our city, the more they contribute to the local economy. Tourism is a huge engine for our economy. And as a place to visit LA has so much to offer the visitor – the climate, the people, the studio tours, the old architecture Downtown... it's very diverse.

The terror attack on September 11 [2001] had a big impact on tourism. Numbers of Japanese visitors, for example, haven't returned to pre-9/11 levels. Every city in America has had the same challenge as us in LA. Another thing that has happened is that people in the United States are travelling more domestically. Our number one domestic market, for example, is people from San Francisco."

49

City parks

The residents of Los Angeles enjoy an open-air lifestyle thanks to the city's pleasant climate. Beach activities are popular all the year round (see page 29). There are also green spaces such as Pershing Square, MacArthur Park and Griffith Park. Pershing Square is the oldest park in Los Angeles. Found in the heart of Downtown, it is home to an ice rink during the winter months. MacArthur Park lies in Koreatown, while Griffith Park is the largest urban park in the United States at around 17 sq km. Situated in the eastern Santa Monica Mountains, it offers residents and visitors the opportunity to go hiking or horseback riding, or to look out from its observatory. For those with enough energy to climb to the top of Mount Hollywood, it also offers sweeping views over the city.

▲ Los Angeles families watch a weekend football league match.

▼ Hiking in Will Rogers State Historic Park is a popular pastime for Los Angeles residents.

Escaping the city

The mountains surrounding Los Angeles are a great escape for the residents of the city. There are many trails for hiking through the canyons of the Santa Monica Mountains. To the east and north of the city the mountains of the Angeles National Forest rise to peaks of over 3,000 metres. The Forest covers over 2,600 sq km and is within an hour's drive for over 20 million people. It offers hiking and mountain biking, fishing and watersports, camping and picnicking, as well as winter sports such as skiing, snow-shoeing and sledging. Another popular escape is Santa Catalina Island, 35 km off the coast, most of which is a nature reserve. It is a popular spot for daytrips from the city.

Looking good

In this city of movie stars and aspiring movie stars, the cult of the body and of good looks is high in importance. Yoga is very popular, and gyms such as Gold's Gym have achieved fame through their well-known clientele (Gold's Gym was where Arnold Schwarzenegger worked out in order to become 'Mr Universe').

Sport

Los Angeles has some of the major names in the US sporting world. The Dodger Stadium is home to the LA Dodgers, the city's main baseball team. Basketball is played at the Staples Center, which is home to the Los Angeles Lakers, the Los Angeles Clippers and the women's team the Los Angeles Sparks. Football (soccer) is very popular with the Hispanic population, and

▲ A skateboarder practises in a Los Angeles park.

has a new home in the Home Depot Center, a huge sports complex that was opened in 2003. It features a 27,000-seater soccer stadium, and is the training headquarters for the national team.

▲ A home game for the Los Angeles Lakers basketball team at the Staples Center.

Los Angeles' environment

Los Angeles is a vast city that uses huge amounts of natural resources, and sends large amounts of emissions into the atmosphere. However, the major environmental issue for the city is one that has dogged it ever since its foundation – water. With an expanding population, the amounts of water needed to keep the city functioning increase every year. Another major issue is air pollution, caused by industry, and by the traffic that clogs the city's streets and freeways.

Water problems

In 2000, the 3.8 million people who obtain their water through the Los Angeles Department of Water and Power (LADWP) used over 830 billion litres in total. Of this amount, over 723 billion litres was brought from sources outside the city. Around 87 per cent of the city's water supply comes from the Colorado River and the Owens Valley (see page 14). The aim for the future of Los Angeles is water conservation. By encouraging people to think about how much water they are using, and by introducing water conservation policies, the LADWP hopes to increase local water supplies. Most of the measures to conserve water are extremely simple: checking pipes for leaks and mending leaky taps, running dishwashers and washing machines with full loads only, and replacing toilets with ultra-low flow flushing models can collectively save millions of litres of water a year.

▼ The Los Angeles Aqueduct carries vital water supplies into the city.

Desalination

Another possible solution to help alleviate the city's water problems is to tap an almost unlimited supply of water – seawater. The LADWP is planning to build the city's first desalination plant at Playa del Ray. The process of converting seawater into drinking water is very expensive, and uses a lot of energy, but once complete the plant will be able to produce about 45 million litres of fresh water per day.

Stormwater

When rain does fall on the city, much of it falls on to hard surfaces such as freeways, pavements and buildings, which do not absorb the water. This water, called runoff, is collected into overflow systems called storm drains. The water in the storm drains is taken directly to the ocean to prevent flooding in the city. However, as the water flows across pavements and other hard surfaces it can become contaminated with pollution, ranging from cigarette butts and animal waste to vehicle oil. None of these pollutants are filtered out before the stormwater is flushed into the sea. LA County is staging a major campaign to make people aware of this problem, and to reduce the amount of pollution on the streets.

Seismic activity

There are about 30 small earthquakes every day in southern California, most of which go unnoticed. But the threat of a major earthquake is something the residents of Los Angeles have to live with. The last devastating earthquake was in 1994 (see page 15), but it is inevitable that another major earthquake will strike the city one day. The City of Los Angeles Emergency Preparedness Department issues guidelines for residents about how to plan for and survive an earthquake, including instructions about preparing a disaster supplies kit and finding cover.

▲ Los Angeles' freeways are at risk from seismic activity. In the 1994 earthquake, sections of major freeways collapsed, closing 11 roads to the city.

◀ Environmental activists protest against water pollution at Santa Monica Bay.

53

Recycling

The City of Los Angeles has an extensive kerbside recycling program, collecting paper, jars, tins, cardboard and plastic containers. It encourages householders to compost their own vegetable and plant waste, and has set up centres for the collection of hazardous waste and e-waste (electronic waste – old computers, televisions etc.). The Council also collects green waste which it composts and resells through the city's nurseries and garden centres. Currently, approximately 45 per cent of residential and 77 per cent of commercial waste in Los Angeles is recycled.

▼ Recycling cans and bottles at one of Los Angeles' many plants.

Air pollution

The extensive use of the car is one of the main contributors to Los Angeles' poor air quality. The geography of the city makes the problem worse as it is surrounded by mountains which trap the polluting smog (see page 22). Air pollution has a major impact on the health of the population, with specific links to asthma, heart disease and lung cancers. In 2005, the greater Los Angeles area came top in a list of the most ozone-polluted areas in the United States. High levels of ozone in the atmosphere can cause symptoms such as shortness of breath, and can damage lung function over a length of time.

The City Council is tackling air pollution in several different ways. It is developing electric-powered and alternative fuel vehicles for public transport around the city to reduce emissions. By the end of 2004, the city was running over 2,000 alternative fuel vehicles, many running on compressed natural gas. In addition, many of the city's police officers now ride bicycles, rather than driving cars. Other strategies include planting trees across the city to provide more natural shade and lower air temperatures, and overhauling facilities such as street lighting to ensure that they use as little energy as possible.

▼ Cars in Los Angeles have compulsory 'smog checks' to evaluate how much their emissions contribute to air pollution in the city.

Detrich B. Allen, General Manager, City of Los Angeles Environmental Affairs Department

"Since the inception in 1990 of the City of Los Angeles Environmental Affairs Department, I have been working with air quality. LA City as a region has the worst air quality in our nation. It is a very big challenge for us. 70 per cent of the pollutants come from mobile sources: cars, buses and so on. These toxins have an impact on public health. The mayor, Antonio Villaraigosa, has a strong green plan for cleaner air. By 2010, for example, we want 20 per cent of the city to be run on renewables. We want to phase out diesel and encourage more hybrid cars by creating a recharging and refuelling infrastructure. Air quality really is the biggest issue here, so everything we do has to deal with it. We've put our police on bicycles, we've got natural gas street sweepers, alternative fuel buses. We're also dealing with it in other ways, building homes and schools. 12 per cent of people in LA can't afford housing. Because house prices have pushed families further away from the jobs in the city centre, there are more and more cars commuting on the road everyday. Our future plan is to create affordable housing so people can move nearer their jobs and cut down on how much they rely on cars."

The Los Angeles of tomorrow

Los Angeles is a city with great vitality. Its amazingly diverse population gives the city a cosmopolitan and creative edge, and its climate and location are two of its great attractions. Yet there are major issues for the future of this huge city.

Housing and the environment

Tackling basic environmental issues such as water supply and air pollution is fundamental to the city's future. Promoting public transport in this city of the car is vital in order to help improve air quality. Housing is another key issue which links in with transport. Providing affordable and decent housing within the city is an extremely high priority for the city council for the future. After the findings of the Housing Crisis Task Force in 2000 (see page 23) the mayor set up the Affordable Housing Trust Fund with an initial fund of US$5 million to pay for affordable housing developments. However, although some progress has been made, waiting lists for affordable housing in the city remain lengthy.

▲ Traffic remains a huge problem in LA, so more and more people are turning to the environmentally friendly option of cycling.

◄ Housing with built-in solar panels for energy conservation. Providing low cost environmentally friendly housing is essential for Los Angeles' future.

Public services and schools

Despite the defeats in the votes of 2002 (see page 39), the issue of secession is unlikely to go away unless the City Council convinces people that it cares as much about the outlying areas of the city as it does about Downtown Los Angeles.

In particular, people are concerned with basic services and the state of the city's schools, and the present mayor, Antonio Villaraigosa, has placed great emphasis on improving schools. Helping those living in poverty in run-down neighbourhoods is another high priority for the future. People on low incomes are often recent immigrants, often working in the 'informal economy' (see page 35) who live on the margins of society. At the same time, its multiethnic society is one of the city's great strengths for the future.

◄ A new school under construction. Schools are vital to the future of Los Angeles.

CASE STUDY

Jesse Alcantae, student, John Monroe High School

"I'm sixteen years old. I'm the fourth child of seven and the first generation of my family to be born outside of Mexico. There is a lot of expectation on me because of this. I was the first born in this land of opportunity, so my family want me to progress. Nobody at home can help me with homework. None of them speak very good English.

My dad is pro-Mexico. He doesn't like it here in America very much. But he also knows that the money is here and that he needs to be here to make it. In this country we can become something. If we stayed in Mexico we would raise cattle or something. Next year I want to go to

university, hopefully an Ivy League (prestigious) one. I want to do accountancy or engineering when I'm older. I want to have my own business."

Glossary

aerospace describes anything to do with rockets, missiles or vehicles that fly in space.

annex to take over.

aqueduct a structure such as a long bridge built to carry water.

Baptist a branch of the Protestant Christian church that believes in adult baptism by total immersion in water.

Buddhist a follower of Buddhism, a religion that originated in India in the 6th century BC, that follows the teachings of the Buddha, the 'enlightened one'.

carpool a lane on a road that is for the use of cars carrying two or more people only.

charter a formal document that outlines the fundamental principles of an organisation.

desalination the process of removing salt from seawater.

evangelical relating to branches of the Christian Church that place emphasis on conversion to Christianity.

federal in the United States describes the national rather than the state government.

firestorm a violent and very dangerous fire, often fanned by strong winds.

freeway a major road that can be used without paying a toll.

Hindu a follower of Hinduism, an Indian religion that has many different gods and goddesses.

Hispanic a term used to describe someone of any race who has their origins in the Spanish-speaking countries of Mexico, Central and South America.

homicide murder or manslaughter.

informal economy describes a wide range of jobs for which workers receive wages in cash and no benefits such as health insurance.

intern to detain or confine someone during wartime.

'Manifest Destiny' the justification for the policy adopted in the 1840s to extend the United States westwards. US leaders saw it as their duty to extend the 'boundaries of freedom' to others through their idealism and belief in democratic institutions.

missionary someone who travels to convert people to their religion.

Muslim a follower of Islam, the religion that has the Qu'ran as its holy book and Muhammad as its most important prophet.

pidgin a language made up from elements of other languages.

poverty level a figure, based on income, below which an individual or family is judged to lack adequate means to live. This figure varies across the world.

pueblo the Spanish word for a settlement.

recession a time of depression in economic activity.

runoff rainfall that runs away as surface water rather than being absorbed by the soil.

secession the act of withdrawing formally from a union or organisation in order to be established separately.

service sector areas are those such as financial services, retail, construction, education, tourism, health care and transportation.

streetcar a tram.

tectonic describes the movement of the plates that form the Earth's crust.

tenement a large house or building that is divided into separate apartments.

Further information

Books to read

Non-fiction

Eyewitness Top 10 Travel Guides Los Angeles Catherine Gerber (Dorling Kindersley, 2006)

The Rough Guide to Los Angeles Jeff Dickey (Rough Guides, 2005)

Fiction

Smoky Night Eve Bunting (Thomson Learning, 1999)

Any Small Goodness: A Novel of the Barrio Tony Johnston (Blue Sky Press, 2001)

Weetzie Bat Francesca Lia Block (HarperCollins, 2004)

Useful websites

http://www.camla.org/index.htm
Website of Chinese American Museum with information about Chinese population in Los Angeles.

http://www.lacity.org/ead/index.htm
City of Los Angeles environmental affairs department

http://www.farmersmarketla.com/index.shtml
Information about Farmers' Markets in Los Angeles

http://www.lacity.org/index.htm
Website for Los Angeles City government

http://lacounty.info
Website for Los Angeles County government

http://www.lacitybeat.com/index.php
Online news from Los Angeles

http://www.ladwp.com/ladwp/homepage.jsp
Website for Los Angeles Department of Power and Water

http://www.lapdonline.org/
Website for Los Angeles Police Department

http://www.laane.org/index.htm
Website for Los Angeles Alliance for a New Economy

http://www.laalmanac.com/default.htm
Facts and figures about Los Angeles County

Index

61

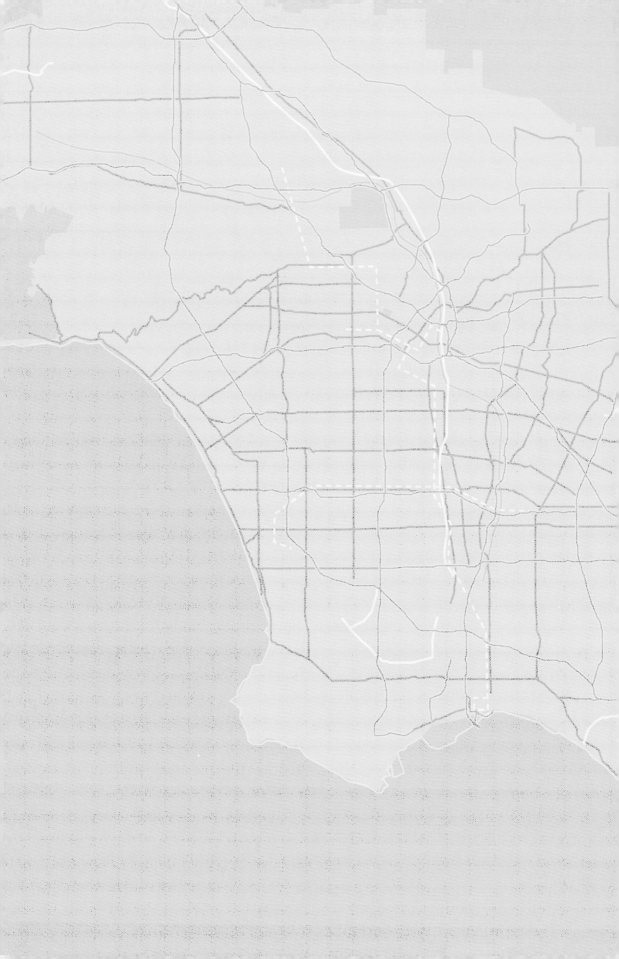